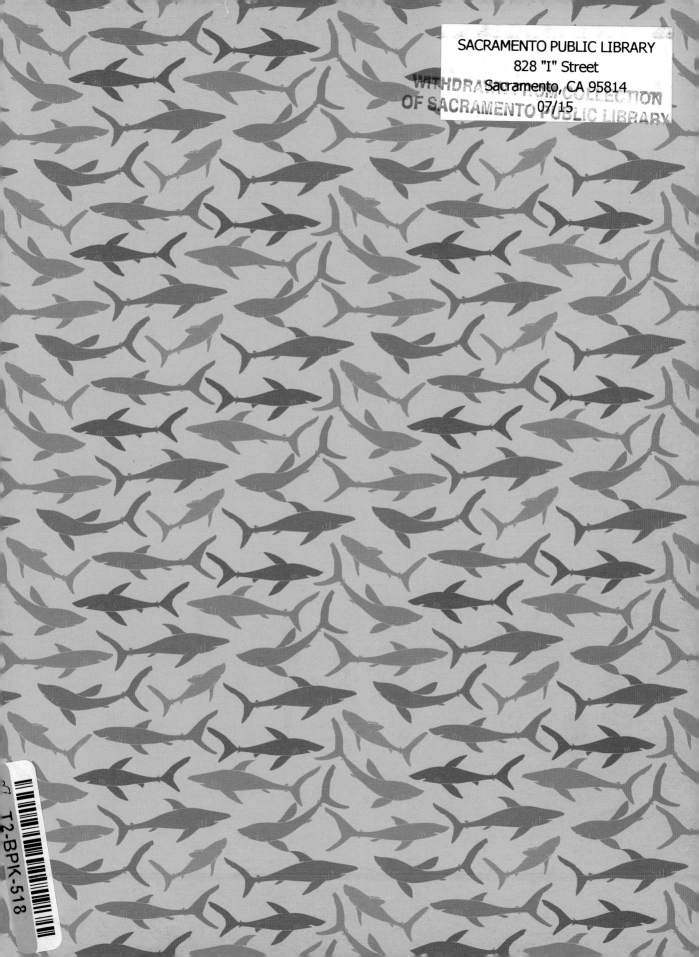

Shark Expedition

SEARCHING FOR GREAT WHITE SHARKS:

A SHARK DIVER'S QUEST FOR MR. BIG

by Mary M. Cerullo

Photographs by Jeffrey L. Rotman

Consultant: James Sulikowski, PhD
Marine Science Department, University of New England

COMPASS POINT BOOKS
a capstone imprint

Compass Point Books are published by Capstone,
1710 Roe Crest Drive, North Mankato, Minnesota 56003
www.capstonepub.com

Editorial Credits
Kristen Mohn, editor; Veronica Scott, designer; Svetlana Zhurkin, media researcher;
Tori Abraham, production specialist

Photo Credits
All phtotographs by Jeffrey L. Rotman with the exception of:
Asher Gal, 1 (bottom), 36 (inset); Isabelle Delafosse, 3, 40 (right); Rodney Fox, 13 (top); Shutterstock:
Alfonso de Tomas, 9, Andreas Meyer, 24, KUCO, 7, Machkazu, 25, Sergey Uryadnikov, 26 (front)
Design Elements by Shutterstock

Library of Congress Cataloging-in-Publication Data
Cerullo, Mary M., author.
Searching for Great white sharks : a shark diver's quest for Mr. Big / by Mary M. Cerullo;
photographs by Jeffrey L. Rotman.
pages cm. — (Compass point books. Shark expedition)
Summary: "Provides information on great white sharks and shares a shark diver's experiences
searching for and photographing them"— Provided by publisher.
Includes index.
 ISBN 978-0-7565-4884-1 (library binding)
 ISBN 978-0-7565-4907-7 (paperback)
 ISBN 978-0-7565-4911-4 (eBook PDF)
1. White shark—Juvenile literature. 2. Rotman, Jeffrey L.—Juvenile literature. 3. Wildlife
photographers—Juvenile literature. 4. Underwater photography—Juvenile literature. I. Title.
QL638.95.L3C468 2015
 597.3'3—dc23   2014006007

For Lydie Driviere, whose friendship and knowledge have meant so much—JLR
For the staff of Friends of Casco Bay, true Friends to the ocean and to me—MMC

Printed in the United States of America in
North Mankato, Minnesota
112014   008604R

TABLE OF CONTENTS

A LIFE UNDERWATER

When people learn that Jeff Rotman is an underwater photographer, they always ask, "How do you keep the sharks away?" Jeff jokes, "The best way to scare a shark away is to jump into the water with a camera!"

A better question for Jeff might be, how do you get the sharks to come to you? He knows from experience that most sharks are timid. Jeff has traveled more than 800,000 miles (1.3 million kilometers) to find and photograph more than 100 different kinds of sharks and rays.

In 40 years of diving, Jeff has found his own ways of coaxing sharks to come to him:

1. Learn their habits—their migration patterns, where they hunt, and how deep they live.

2. Wait—sometimes for a very ... long ... time.

3. Offer treats. (Their favorite foods are fish heads and squashed sardines.)

"Being a good diver is the number one requirement for being a shark photographer. Even so, don't get so comfortable underwater that you forget where you are," Jeff warns. "Never underestimate the shark or overestimate your diving ability."

A diver feeds sharks to get them to pose for photos.

MR. BIG

If you asked Jeff to name his favorite shark, he wouldn't hesitate: a great white. "There is no other shark that can match a great white shark in size, personality, and power," he said. "It's the only shark I've ever seen that sticks its head out of the water and looks right at you." Scientists believe great whites likely developed this behavior to spy on sea lions sunning themselves on the rocks. Jeff says that when one stares at you with those huge black eyes, "you know that it is checking you out."

Jeff refers to the great white as Mr. Big. "Where other sharks are sleek, this one is brawny, like a football player." Its size and strength help a great white shark bring down a hefty adversary, such as a sea lion or an elephant seal. Imagine being chased down by a predator as big as the family car.

GREAT WHITE SHARK STATS

AVERAGE LENGTH:
15 feet (4.6 meters)

MAXIMUM LENGTH:
21 feet (6.4 m)

MAXIMUM WEIGHT:
5,000 pounds (2,268 kilograms)

RANGE:
most often found in cool coastal waters,
but they roam worldwide

LIFE SPAN:
about 30 years

DIET:
fish, squid, dolphins, sea turtles, fur seals,
elephant seals, sea lions, whale calves,
and dead whales

FOLLOW THE FOOD

To find a shark, you must go where the food is. Great white sharks prefer blubbery sea lions, seals, and dead or dying whales. Eating plump prey can sustain a great white for weeks or even a month. Between meals it can live off the fat stored in its liver.

The fur and blubber of these prey marine mammals keep them warm in cold seas. And eating the blubber provides the energy that great whites need to digest their food quickly. It also makes their muscles react fast enough to catch quick swimmers such as seals and dolphins.

GUADALUPE ISLAND

Great white sharks know the best hunting spots are where seals, sea lions, and other marine mammals have their young.

A Galápagos sea lion does a backflip for the camera.

Scientists have learned that great whites can travel far to find their favorite foods. At various times of the year, you can find them in different parts of the world:

February to April
Dangerous Reef, Australia, to eat sea lions

May to September
Dyer Island and Seal Island, South Africa, to eat Cape fur seals

August to December
Guadalupe Island, Mexico, to eat northern elephant seals, California sea lions, and Guadalupe fur seals

Sharks don't have blubber. So how do great whites cope with the chilly water? Unlike cold-blooded fish, which take on the temperature of the surrounding water, great white sharks can raise and maintain their body temperature so that it's warmer than the water around them.

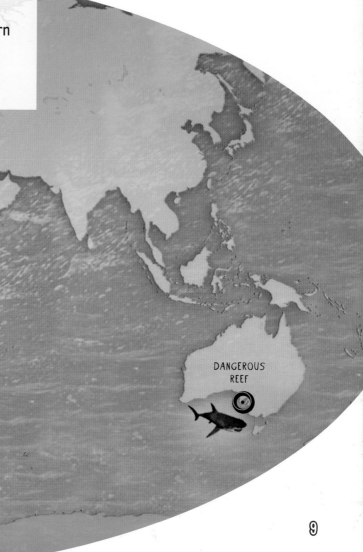

SEAL
ISLAND
DYER
ISLAND

DANGEROUS
REEF

Divers have to stay warm too. Like most divers, Jeff wears a wetsuit that covers him from head to toe. A little bit of seawater seeps inside the suit when he enters the water. His body warms the water, because humans are warm-blooded, maintaining a constant body temperature of 98.6°F (37°C). But after a while, the surrounding water, even in tropical seas, draws the warmth away. Then Jeff has to take a break to get warmed up on the deck of the boat.

Fish don't have eyelids, but many sharks have special coverings that slide over their eyes when they attack. The coverings protect them from the sharp claws of a fur seal or the tusks of an elephant seal.

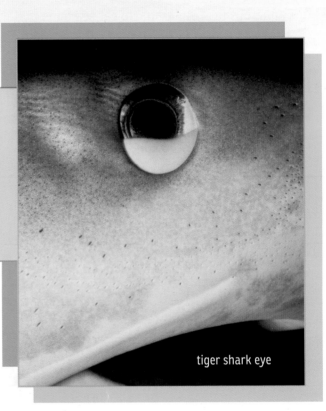

tiger shark eye

whitetip reef shark skin

FACT:

A shark doesn't feel like other fish. Instead of scales, its body is covered with denticles that give the skin a rough, sandpapery feel. A shark's skin is made from the same material as its teeth. All the denticles point backward, so if you were to run your hand along a shark from snout to tail, it would feel smooth. If you rubbed it the other way—ouch! A tough hide is one way that a shark protects itself in the ocean.

MAKE LIKE A FISH

Jeff knows he must look odd to other underwater creatures. No fish requires so much equipment or has air bubbles gurgling up from a scuba tank. In order to make sharks comfortable with him—and to make himself comfortable in their world—Jeff works hard to become more like a fish.

- Flippers act like fins for swimming, turning, or staying upright in the water.

- Instead of gills, Jeff has an air tank to breathe underwater.

- Goggles imitate a shark's glassy eyeballs.

- A wetsuit not only keeps Jeff warm—it helps to protect him if he scrapes against rocks, corals, or the rough skin of a shark.

- Jeff's knife acts like a shark's teeth and can be used to free him from a fishing net if needed.

JEFF'S FIRST ENCOUNTER
DANGEROUS REEF, AUSTRALIA

For many years Jeff dreamed of photographing a great white shark. Although great white sharks are found worldwide, they are not common anywhere.

Jeff knew if anyone could help him find a great white shark, it would be Australian conservationist Rodney Fox.

Few people understand great whites better than this man, who survived a great white shark attack. Despite the attack, he has become one of the champions working to protect these animals. And they need protection—scientists estimate there are only about 200 great whites left along Australia's southern coast.

RODNEY'S GREAT WHITE RUN-IN

Rodney Fox is perhaps the most famous shark attack victim ever. As a young man, he was attacked by a great white during a spearfishing contest. He barely survived. Doctors pieced him back together like a jigsaw puzzle, using 462 stitches and 6 pints (2.8 liters) of blood.

After the attack Rodney hated great white sharks and wanted to kill them all. In time, though, he realized that they are important predators in the ocean. Sharks target prey that is easy to catch, such as sick, weak, or dying animals. Rodney calls great whites "the great feeding and cleaning machines of the deep."

Today Rodney takes scientists and photographers to meet great white sharks so that they can understand them better and educate others. Rodney also tracks the numbers of great whites in southern Australia. He tags them so they can be identified when they are seen in other places and in other years. He recognizes many sharks by sight, identifying them by their color patterns or notches in their fins.

Despite almost being killed by a great white shark, Rodney Fox is one of the biggest protectors of the species.

Rodney Fox today holding pictures of himself after the attack

February, March, and April are summer months in Australia. That is when great white sharks come to visit, so that was the perfect time for Jeff to visit too. Jeff journeyed to a place in southern Australia called Dangerous Reef, to join an expedition led by Rodney and Rodney's son Andrew. Also on this trip was famous filmmaker Stan Waterman, who was shooting a movie on great white sharks called *Blue Water, White Death*.

Once aboard their dive boat on Dangerous Reef, Rodney mixed up a secret recipe of blood, horsemeat, and fish parts. Andrew ladled this "chum" from a large tub into the water, leaving a trail of smells that called to the sharks like a dinner bell.

Andrew Fox making chum

FACT:

Great whites have a keen sense of smell. They can detect even one drop of blood in 10 billion drops of water.

As the photographers pulled on their scuba tanks, the boat's crew finished tying tuna heads to the sides of the shark cages. The divers stepped from the boat into three large cages floating at the surface. Then the crew let out the lines so the cages would drift away from the boat, allowing the divers to watch for sharks from every direction.

They watched.

And waited.

Sometimes they waited in the boat, sometimes in the water. Jeff says, "Much of wildlife photography is waiting."

"A cage is a must when diving with great white sharks," Jeff says. "Being in a shark cage reverses the whole zoo experience. You become the animal behind the bars."

After about five hours, they saw a shape appear 50 to 60 feet (15 to 18 m) away. Jeff immediately realized that this was different from any other shark he'd ever seen. It did not move cautiously. It came straight toward them at a steady pace. As it got nearer, they realized how enormous it was. It yanked a tuna head off the side of the cage and vanished.

Hearts beating fast, the divers stared in the direction the shark had disappeared. For what seemed like a very long 15 minutes, nothing happened. Then the shark barreled into the other side of the cage and grabbed another tuna.

Jeff had just witnessed how great white sharks attack their prey. They sneak up from below and behind to ambush their victims in surprise attacks.

FACT:

Sample biting is how scientists describe the feeding behavior of great white sharks. They take a sample, and if it's good, they come back for more.

The next morning five great white sharks circled the cages. What an experience! Jeff knew that many divers never get to see one great white, let alone five.

Over the next 10 days, the divers spent many hours watching the sharks feed and snapping photos. Every day it was the same pattern. The largest shark would come to the cage first to feed on tuna heads, while the others waited 50 to 70 feet (15 to 21 m) away. Once the first left, the next largest shark would approach, following a pecking order.

From sunup to sundown, the divers would go into the cages for an hour and a half, come out for an hour, and go back in for two hours. After so many hours standing in 55°F (12.8°C) water, the divers never warmed up, even after they got back on the boat. Each day they had to add more layers to their wetsuits.

Jeff recalls his impressions of his first meeting with great whites. *"I was stunned by their size and power and how differently they behaved from other sharks. With most other sharks, I could imagine defending myself from an attack. With a white, I quickly realized that if this shark decides you are lunch, there is really nothing you can do about it."*

"When photographing great white sharks, never stick your hand or head outside the cage," advises Jeff. "That may seem obvious, but I have seen professionals do it. You may think there is only one shark out there, but other sharks could be lurking. And they have a knack for approaching on your blind side. Some photographers are so focused on filming the shark that they forget that one good chomp could be the end of their career!"

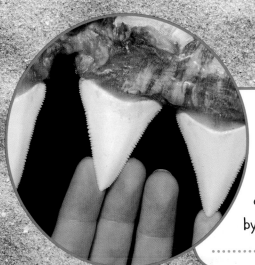

FACT:

Great white sharks have about 25 triangular teeth arranged in several rows. Like saw blades, their teeth easily slice off huge hunks of flesh. Some shark experts can identify the kind of shark just by its teeth, or even by the wounds the teeth leave in a shark attack victim.

HYPNOTIZING SHARKS
DYER ISLAND, SOUTH AFRICA

Jeff heard about another shark buff who seemed to be able to make sharks obey his command. Jeff had to see this for himself, so he went to Gansbaai, South Africa, to visit Andre Hartman, known as the shark wrangler.

Andre is a former spearfishing champion of South Africa. During one contest Andre was swimming back to the boat with his catch when a great white shark tried to make Andre *his* prize. Andre pushed the shark away with his spear gun, and the shark fled.

Another time, Andre was working on his dive boat when a great white tried to bite the outboard motor. Worried that the

Andre Hartman (far left) has a way with great whites.

shark would hurt his boat (and itself), Andre reached over the side to push the shark away. As he touched its snout with his hand, the shark suddenly leapt out of the water and opened its mouth as if to snap Andre up. But instead of trying to bite Andre, the shark slid harmlessly back into the sea.

Andre figured that he had accidentally overloaded the shark's sensory organs that detect the electricity generated by its surroundings. It was as if he'd put the shark into a trance. Andre repeated this feat with many other great white sharks and became famous for it.

FACT:

A shark has a special sense contained in pores along its jaw and snout called ampullae of Lorenzini. It detects the electrical field that radiates from every living thing (and many metallic objects).

21

When Jeff arrived in South Africa, Andre explained that the weather, wind, and water conditions had to be just right in order for Jeff to capture the image of the "hypnotized shark." For the next four weeks, as Jeff waited for the perfect day, he interviewed people with knowledge of great whites, photographed other sea life of the region, and read lots of books.

Finally, on the last day of Jeff's trip, the sea was calm. Andre exclaimed, "It's time!" They sped off in his motorboat to Dyer Island.

Andre stood on a step at the back of the boat and tossed out a shark liver tied to a rope. On cue a great white leaped to grab the bait. Andre reached over and touched its nose. The shark opened its mouth as wide as a patient in the dentist's chair.

"After 31 days of waiting, the shot took only 3 or 4 minutes," says Jeff. "Sometimes you have to wait a long time to get that one great photograph."

AIR JAWS
SEAL ISLAND, SOUTH AFRICA

Jeff wanted to investigate another amazing great white shark behavior he'd heard about at False Bay, South Africa. He met up with ocean guides Chris and Monique Fallows. Chris and a friend had discovered that great white sharks can breach like whales, jumping right out of the water to capture fur seals.

Jeff visited at the time of year when Cape fur seals give birth on nearby Seal Island, because that's when the great whites come for the seal meals. They hunt there until the pups and their parents leave.

In order to get to their feeding grounds, the seals have to get past the sharks lurking just beyond the shoreline. In groups of five to 20, the adult and young seals leap into the water from a rocky ledge that locals call The Launch Pad. They make a mad dash for their feeding grounds outside the bay, relying on safety in numbers. After a few days feeding at sea, they return to shore. It's on the return trip to the island, when seals are swimming back alone or in small groups, that the danger is greatest. On average, the seal colony loses seven seals a day to hungry sharks.

Where there is a colony of fur seals and their pups, you can be sure great whites are nearby.

More than half the successful attacks on seals happen around sunrise. From below, the sharks can see the seals against the brightening sky, but the seals have a hard time making out the dark back of a great white shark swimming below them. To catch a seal, a great white explodes out of the water in a burst of speed scientists estimate at about 20 miles (32 km) an hour. Sometimes they jump as high as 10 feet (3 m) into the air.

The shark attacks its prey with a wide-open mouth that watchers call "Air Jaws." But if the shark misses on its first try, the seal just might get away. It may leap right over the head of the shark, escaping the giant jaws by inches. However the chase ends, it is sure to be a fur-raising experience for the seal.

A Cape fur seal narrowly escapes a great white.

A great "white" shark is really only white underneath. Its back is darker gray. This pattern is called countershading.

A great white shark is one of the only sharks that
can leap out of the water in pursuit of prey.

About 60,000 Cape fur seals live on Seal Island during the pupping season, so it would seem that Jeff would have many chances to see a seal-shark encounter. But most of the hunting takes place underwater, which is not a safe place to be without a cage.

So the Fallows have devised a way to get sharks to jump on cue. They construct a seal decoy, which they tow behind a boat to tempt a great white to leap up and grab it. The Fallows have been successful in getting great white sharks to perform this action hundreds of times. Of course, they have to replace their decoy seals often.

Since 1996 the Fallows have been leading ecotourism trips to give visitors a chance to witness the amazing athletic behavior of great white sharks. They also collaborate on many research projects that help scientists learn more about shark behavior. And of course they give photographers such as Jeff the opportunity to catch a shark midair.

A great white breaches to attack a seal decoy.

A GREAT WHITE BUFFET
GUADALUPE ISLAND, MEXICO

In a place where tasty elephant seals, fur seals, and sea lions all gather to have their pups, great white sharks won't be far behind. From August through early December, tourists and underwater photographers are almost sure to find great white sharks lurking in the waters near Guadalupe Island off the coast of Mexico.

Jeff found that the great white sharks there are not as big as the ones he photographed in Australia. Most are about 11 feet (3.4 m) long, instead of 18 feet (5.5 m). But they are plenty big enough for the tourists who view them from cages suspended from dive boats.

Jeff explains that the bars of an aluminum cage won't prevent a great white from tearing it apart. Instead, the shark's electric sense detects a boundary that the shark usually won't cross. But there are exceptions. On rare occasions a shark gets so excited that it rushes at the cage. If a great white gets stuck between the bars of the cage, it panics and thrashes around as the divers cower in the corner. The shark tears apart the cage to free itself. All escape and the tourists go home with an amazing story of how they spent their vacation!

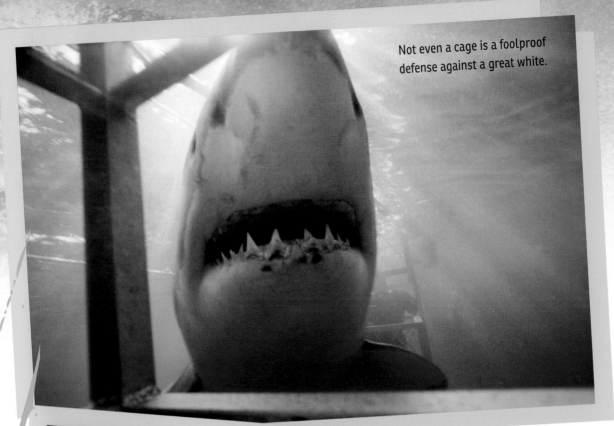

Not even a cage is a foolproof defense against a great white.

During his trip to Guadalupe Island, Jeff wanted to learn how far great whites would travel in search of food. Those are questions that shark scientists want to answer too. To learn about shark migration, they attach electronic tags to the dorsal fins of great whites. The tags send information from the sharks up to satellites circling Earth and back down to the researchers' labs. Information about where the sharks go and how deep they dive is relayed to computers. One great white traveled 12,000 miles (19,000 km) from South Africa to Australia and back in nine months.

The electronic tags show that many great white sharks swim out to the middle of the Pacific Ocean to an area that scientists have named the White Shark Café. The café is visited by great whites from Guadalupe, Mexico, and from along the northern California coast, around the Farallon Islands and Año Nuevo. They stay there for about three months, hunting squid, swordfish, and other sharks.

Experts aren't sure what draws the great whites all the way to the café. But the food there must make the long trip worthwhile; scientists who have tracked great white sharks from Guadalupe and back report that they return home looking well fed.

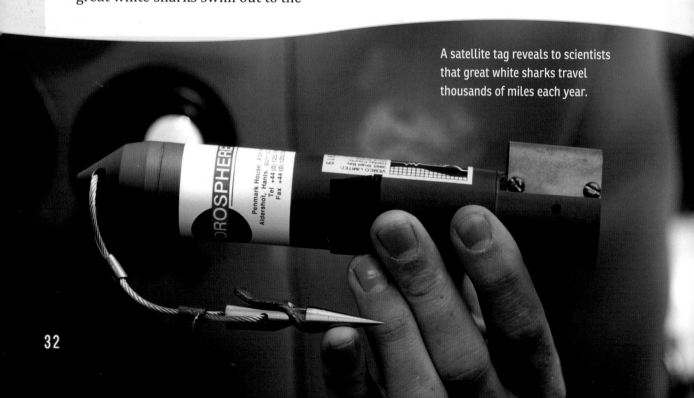

A satellite tag reveals to scientists that great white sharks travel thousands of miles each year.

FACT:

Generally great whites feed near the surface during the daytime. But they often dive much deeper, likely in search of prey. Satellite tags have shown that great whites may dive as deep as 4,000 feet (1,200 m).

HOW PEOPLE FEEL ABOUT GREAT WHITES

For years after the movie *Jaws* came out, many people refused to go swimming in the ocean because they were afraid they might run into a great white shark. In some seaside communities where there had never been a shark attack, police had to patrol the beaches to reassure swimmers that it was safe to go into the water. Great whites were stalked by big-game trophy hunters. Their teeth, jaws, and preserved bodies were valuable prizes.

Now concern for great whites is growing, and many people want to get as close as they can to great whites. But the sharks are getting harder to find. Even though great whites aren't caught for food, as many other sharks are, they still are hunted for sport in some places. Others are caught by accident in fishing nets. Great whites are listed as a "vulnerable" species, meaning that declining populations in many parts of the world are bringing them closer to extinction. Many countries now have laws to protect great whites and help increase their populations worldwide.

Shark teeth jewelry shows how variable shark teeth can be.

THE LEGACY OF *JAWS*

In 1975 a blockbuster movie called *Jaws* played in theaters. It was about a great white shark attacking swimmers at a popular beach. The movie scared people so much that there was a rush to kill great whites (and any other sharks). Stories of attacks still make the news and cause fear, but your chances of being eaten by a shark are only about one in 300 million. You have an equal chance of being killed by falling airplane parts.

About 100 shark attacks are reported worldwide each year. A third to a half of those are blamed on great whites. You might think that all great white shark attacks would be fatal, but most are not. After a sample bite, great whites usually release humans. But that first nibble can cause serious damage.

Shark conservationists like Rodney and Andrew Fox, Andre Hartman, and Chris and Monique Fallows are calling for more laws to protect great whites. These people work around sharks on a daily basis and have a great respect for these top predators. They are working to set aside more areas of the ocean as marine sanctuaries. They are encouraging more ecotourism in order to fund the sanctuaries and to help the public understand great whites.

Underwater photographer Jeff Rotman is surrounded by the tools of his trade.

Whenever there is an attack on a human by a great white shark, some people call for changes in laws to allow great whites to be hunted. Jeff Rotman feels differently. "You have to share the ocean with these animals," he says. "You do take a risk in some areas of the ocean. But you won't fix that by killing every great white shark."

After all, we're visitors in their world. And Jeff will keep visiting and photographing their world to share its wonders with those of us above sea level.

GLOSSARY

ampullae of Lorenzini—pores on the snouts of sharks and rays containing sensors that detect weak electric currents

cold-blooded—having a body temperature that changes with the surrounding temperature

dorsal fin—a fin located on the back

ecotourism—visiting a place that has unspoiled natural resources, while being careful to have minimal impact on the environment

marine sanctuary—a section of the ocean where a government has placed limits on human activities to protect the habitat and marine life

migration—the periodic seasonal movement of animals from one geographic region to another

pecking order—an animal behavior where one animal demonstrates it has a higher status among its kind by actions such as eating first or taking the best resting place

satellite tag—a radio tag attached to an animal that allows scientists to track its movements by sending a signal to satellites orbiting Earth

scuba—self-contained underwater breathing apparatus, based on the device developed by Emile Gagnan and Jacques Cousteau, which uses a tank of compressed gas (usually air) for diving

warm-blooded—having a body temperature that stays about the same all the time

READ MORE

Discovery Channel. *The Big Book of Sharks.*
New York: Time Home Entertainment, 2012.

Civard-Racinais, Alexandrine. *Great White Shark:
Myth and Reality.* Richmond Hill, Ont.: Firefly Books, 2012.

Riehecky, Janet. *Great White Sharks: On the Hunt.*
Mankato, Minn.: Capstone Press, 2009.

INTERNET SITES

Use FactHound to find Internet sites related to this book.
All of the sites on FactHound have been researched by our staff.

Here's all you do:

Visit *www.facthound.com*

Type in this code:
9780756548841

AUTHOR

Mary M. Cerullo has been teaching and writing about the ocean and natural history for 40 years. She has written more than 20 children's books on ocean life. Mary is also associate director of the conservation organization Friends of Casco Bay/Casco Baykeeper in Maine, where she lives with her family.

Mary with granddaughter Taylor

PHOTOGRAPHER

Jeffrey L. Rotman is one of the world's leading underwater photographers. Diving and shooting for more than 40 years—and in nearly every ocean and sea in the world—this Boston native combines an artist's eye with a naturalist's knowledge of his subjects. His photography has been featured on television and in print worldwide. Jeff and his family live in New Jersey.

Jeff with sons Matthew and Thomas

INDEX

BEACH 50m

SURFING

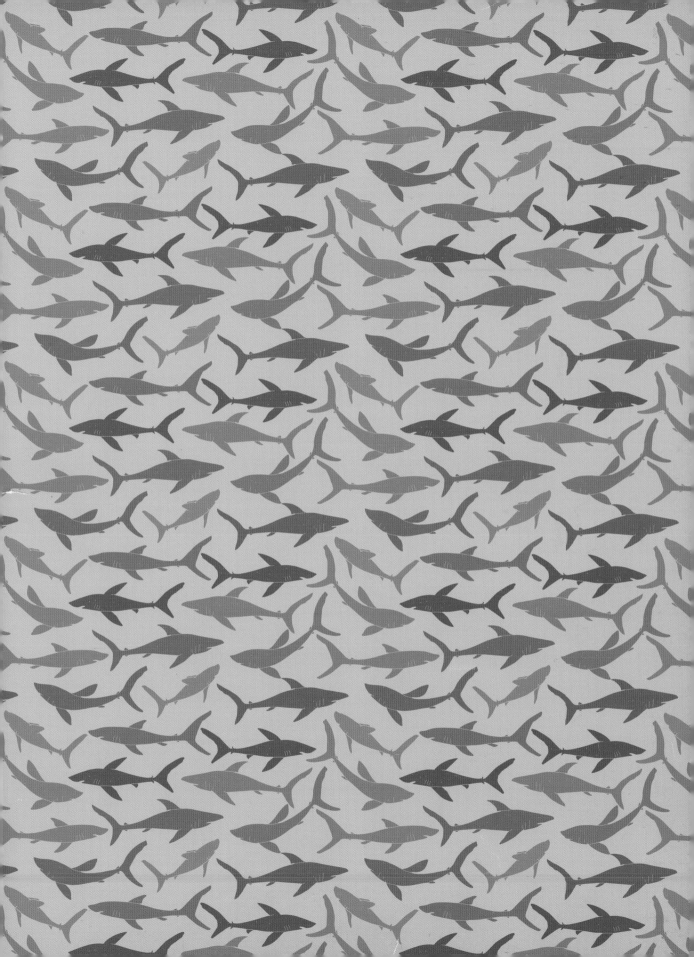